Perspective

Is The

Objective

Logan Gregoire

Foreword

This world has come a long way since the idea of day and creation of word. With the evolution of technology to bring us both closer together from even further reaches around this world. It has driven us further apart as a society and separated the actual person from their own body and consciousness which is where the greatest loss of this world lies.

Inside each individual where internal happiness is lost for lack of perspective or because of the comparison of others and what their situation might hold or how another's actions have impacted your situation. Lack of understanding and perspective is what brings out very strong uncontrolled emotions that are lost. These emotions must be cautiously analyzed by each individual for we cannot change another's actions, only have a presence of mind to understand the greater flow of a situation and the possible reasons to their intentions.

 Not every person is thinking about how their choices can impact another's but you yourself can be aware of not only what's around you but possible perspective's to allow others to flow quickly through your area in a calm, graceful manner even if the others actions are considered unthoughtful.

Copyright © 2020 by Logan Gregoire

All rights reserved. No part of this publication or its accompanying materials may be reproduced, scanned, or distributed in any printed or electronic form without written permission

Table of Contents

"The Table Of Grand Champions"

"Where The Feet Meet"

"Tap Into A Silhouette"

"In It For The Long Haul"

"A Bunch Of Tough Cookies"

"Sounds That Make No Notes"

"Simple Fix"

"The Other Side Of Tomorrow"

"To Find The Fountain"

"Dawn"

"One Day"

"Control A Nightmare If They Dare"

"The New World"

"Ex's And Oh's"

"To Look Outside The Light"

"The Mist"

"Stay"

"Never Really Behind"

"Perspective Is The Objective"

"More Like Fiction Each Day"

"Snooze"

"Back Up To Five"

"Reflection On The Connection"

"Left Better On Paper"
"Tik Tok"
"City Of Black And White"
"The Movement"
"Define A Black Hole"
"To Diagnose A Personality"
"As They Please"
"Fiction Is History"
"The Static"
"Judgement"
"7th Sense"
"Are You Still In There?"
"Slysdexic"
"Cut The Line"
"Smirk Behind A Smile"
"To Weave The Sands Of Time"
"Black Or White"
"The Application"
"When It's Sunny And Snowing"
"The Curtain Falls"
"PeEk A BoO"

"The Table of Grand Champions"

There is a table where each cherished adventurer is whole heartedly grateful for the places they've been.
Where the legendary laced seats are reserved onLy for the willfully genuine,
The greatest conqueror's all know what perspective is and can say it with an inspirational grin,
For their ability to notice is what allows them to continually win.

This is the table where the greatest of all dIsciplines can relax and reflect,
Since each battle that is fought is with all the devoted knowledge from their life and mastered suBject,
As each warrior has rightfully earned their place by admirably carrying the flame of mighty mutual respect.

These peaceful warriors continue fighting for the others who have no mental peacE.
They need not carry any physical armor since their coverings are woven of nothing but fleece.

It is the table of gRand champions where all the walks of life can reside,
For the idea of black and white is no longer a concept to divide.
This single thought is hard to brave yet it is always carried with the utmost of pride.

To obtain a chair one must be courTeous and kind,
Even in the presence of one who is prospectively blind.
This is the ultimate test of every powerful passing mind.

One must never reply to a task with a negative grumble,
As they've learned to sustain the thought of always being humble,
While alwaYs offering a helping hand when another person has taken a tumble.

"Where the Feet Meet"

Welcome to this place called planet earth,
It's alWays been this way since the day of birth.

Life's a battle to see who's the baddest in the land,
Only until there's no more blood in the gland.

Some want to play,
While other say that's okay.
Everyone fIghts until the end of day,
And it's a dog eat dog world, so choose predator or prey.

Pick your battle, mental or physical,
Go with the path that seems most intrinsical.

It's always a delight to go pound for pound,
But take a good look around,
And you'll see that we all eventualLy become a part of the ground.

The circle of life can onLy be complete,
When we all gather where the feet meet.

"Tap into a Silhouette"

People see the color and think of what darkness lurks near,
As the shadow is depicted as the spellcasters darkest fear.
The reality is an everlasting playground that sends light bursts through the winds that are indescribably clear.
It delivers messages so stRong and beautiful that the performer need only drop a single tear.

Once one understands the attack of angle on light,
Then can they lace their illuminating energy for the opposIng dark matter fight.
The shadows blade is so energetically strong that it disappears out of sight,
In the midst of the performaNce it will emit a direct reflection that hovers over the night,
For it contains another colors edge so sharp as it slashes through the black and white.

Each strike creates a glistening world of colors that are slightly offset,
Then bursts a universe of opposing forces that contain unity guidelines that must gracefully be met.
The state of conscious mind is easy to forGet,
As the other lost light practice is to tap into a silhouette.

"In It for The Long Haul"

This life can sometimes feel lonesome and that's perFectly okay,
Our strong muscles and bones are shouting out that we're here to stay.
Even if we are housing the prehistoric birds of prey.

It's much like a lonely white pine growing high and mighty on a rocky mountain side.
The challenges are excruciating and the elements we can't decide.
However, there is still a shelter that we are able to pRovide,
Adapt to this idea and the internal battles shall no longer collide.

The going of life can be intimidating and prEtty tough,
As we overlook the canyon and think that others lives just aren't as rough.
Just know that some weren't built for this kind of stuff.

To allow the ability to grow so high and mighty tall,
We must not be afraid of shedding some previously living needles on that steep cliffsidE fall.
As well as understand, that we are all in it for the long haul.

"A Bunch of Tough Cookies"

Sometimes life's a competition of hoW far we can throw,
Or simply having the greatest mind to win an intelligence show.
Certainly, there is still one thing to know,
Even the toughest or smartest of man contains a piece of his heart that is soft as dougH.

The variety of flavors and sizes we come in are wide and plentiful.
Underneath our regenerating skin is one pretty tough skull,
As we are all created from a genetic code that was once considered a solid whole.
Now remember each and every one of us contains a different life goal,
And even the craziest of extremes can seem like somEone else's version of dull.

Even if we are children for the first time learning the ABC's,
Or possibly someone who has spent a lifetime beatiNg up their knees.
Somewhere there is an expert teaching the up and coming rookies,
As the fact will always remain that we are all just a bunch of tough cookies.

"Sounds That Make No Notes"

When ecstatically expressing thyself in the presence of a moment,
as if dancing in thE moonlight upon Saturn's rings,
There are those showstopping captures of time that the memory will always bring.
All the way back to the day when the energetic soul hAd its own song to sing.
As the peaceful warrior once wielded his armor and the beautiful love arrows specially crafted to sling,
And then carefully fired away by a powerful bow with all of his heart for the string.

The energy transmitted sent electricity through the air,
It would eventually create a smile that read, treat deliCately with only the utmost giving care.
As I have only one crazy lifetime that I'm willing to share,
Yet I've still got to light up the world like a beautiful cosmic flare.

To fly together there wasn't a need to have any approval votes.
For when we sHared the moment, the universe celebrated time as if it was the most beautiful of parade floats.
That's because we proved capable of generating the sounds that make no notes.

"Simple Fix"

Oh, if life was just a simple fix,
We'd all have our own book of tricks.

However, there is no medication,
For personal dedication,
As this often leads to internal frustration.

See the game of life is just a trial,
Since we all have our own vision of a hyPnotic style.
So, take your mind just outsidE the vial,
And things might change once in a while.

It's haRd to be a pioneer,
When the mind doesn't see clear.

So look behind the eye,
And ask yourself why,
"Why, oh why hasn't your soul been sent to fly?"

The anSwer is inside,
Where ideas collide,
And the truth dOes reside.

Take a dose of your own medication,
Play life as if you're the leader of motivation,
To ingrain the thoughts of personal dedication.

This really is the simple fix,
For eNding all conflicts.

"The Other Side of Tomorrow"

What comes and goes,
No one knows.
It's why peopLe get scared when there's a flock of crows.

Travel to the land whEre it doesn't matter who has that or this,
It is only then will you find internal bliss.

When life is treated as an eternAl discovery,
There is no need for mental recovery.

So, if you do so choose to follow,
It's beyond the realm of sleepy hollow.
Where there isn't room for the softest of soRrow,
Or the saNds of time for people to borrow.
It simply is being part of the other Side of tomorrow.

"To Find the Fountain"

I have found the place of youth,
Many have been searching as if it was in a booth.
However, it's a place of unspeakable truth.

You cannoT use a footstep riser,
To get past the crystal geyser.

In this place there are no numbers,
As everything here takes rest in the eternal slumbers.

Many lives had lost their mind,
Simply because they led on too hard a grind,
Only for a search to never find.

This does not lie inside a mystical mOuntain,
But if one wants to find the only youth fountain,
It rests behind the days that people aren't countin'.

"Dawn"

You get to choose as the sun starts to rise,
If you will no longer hear the mournful cries,
As if existence has been wiped of all its lies.
So, take your heart and seeing eyeS,
And place them high into the rising skies.

It's a new beginning to the living earth,
Some would even consider it a visible rebirth.

Welcome to dawn,
Where all the problEms are gone,
And the newest of ideas come to a spawn.

It gives the soul the grandest of rEason to run,
That's when the being is chasing the colorful rising sun.

"One Day"

"One day, one day…"
It's what the people say.
It leads to a liFe where they wander astray,
Not enjoying the jOys of going out to play.
The being eventually starts to fRay,
As the people continue to say,
"It'll get done, one day."

"Control a Nightmare if They Dare"

As every moment is in a sTate of change,
It brings simple emotions to an even broader range,
While every being is making an energy exchange.

It will most certainly get the heart to jump,
Then the blood starts to erratically pump,
And tears begin to helplessly dump.

To some it may be tHeir own darkest fear,
Or when the presence of another threatening being is near.
However, I must say this moment is when the mind is genuinely seeing clear.

It will take you to the edge of your seam,
Much like trying to conquer the high beam,
But a nightmare is still a living dream.
Once it's controllEd, the mind and body become a unified team.

In order to produce that mystical stare,
That is capable of saying, "We've both been there."
One must control a nightmare,
If they dare.

"The New World"

Would your idea of life have ever been sustained,
If it was based purely on the thoughts you've gathered and obtained,
Or would the universe itself get ever so gently drained?

When you see what I envision as well and have Previously sought to chasing it too,
Then there is a progressive convErsation that has no further a due.

Now it'd be only us running around in this stampede,
So we needn't to hit each other at a catastrOphic warp speed.
It's an elegantly beautiful process as the transaction is guaranteed to succeed.

In the word's strength, hoPe, and progress we hail.
From the darkest of gloom, we can all prevail,
As natures color changing dust has diminished the last traveling light rail.

There is a bond that can be created that sustains more grip than the toughest of steel that's been knurled.
It would be possibLe to harness the harshest of winds that get twirled,
Or even tap into the great forces of water that get swirled.
There wouldn't be any weight that couldn't be curled,
For this would be what we envision as the creation of the nEw world.

"Ex's and Oh's"

Even in times of the harshest blizzard,
There is a thought that will turn you into a social wizard.

The storm may had come hArd,
But it will eventually water a beautiful blossoming yard.

If you played the card too early,
It was probably because you thought your mind was beyond burly.

It's not until the light bulb goes flick,
That the mind undeRstands what makes the being tick.

The lessons of life, they come and go,
For everything that once was is now a new thing to know.

So, just when you had it figured out and an idEa to a close,
Just remember there will always be more Ex's and Oh's.

"To Look Outside the Light"

You can look at, or you can look through.
The simple question will alWays be who,
All while acting on a stage fit just fOr you.

There simply is no need to care.
As you're now performing foR the beings that live beyond the air,
While expressing yourself in a manner you can share.

Slow your breath, then go fasteR.
Only then can you calm the winds of disaster.

The magic doesn't happen,
Until the fingers are a snappin',
While the toes are a tappin',
And you're not worrIed if the people are a clappin'.

Forget what it's like to fEel a fright,
Perform as if it were the miDdle of the night,
When there's not a single being ever in sight.
This is what it's like to look outside the light.

"The Mist"

All options exist,
When stAnding in the mist.

It's a place where you can Build,
And all your dreams are fulfilled.

Attract all your desires,
And you could craft empires.

This place is sO crazy,
Because it's so hazy.

YoU can lift the veil,
To let the mind sail.

It's a place to transcend,
But it seems to have no end.

The idea is sentimental,
For it's all in the menTal.

Just remember all options exist,
Because the mind is the mist.

"Stay"

Every bull is looking for a person to hire,
For the life is caught building another's empire.
This continuously adds fuel to the fire.
Now that life is spent Waiting to retire,
All while chasing a personal desire.

It's easy to chase a life of security,
Yet it burns away at the soul's purity.

These feelings only create strife,
As the individual is no longer living life.
It always cuts way deeper tHan any other knife.

It's only a matter of time,
Before one realizes thAt it's all for a dime,
This takes away from a life that is genuinely sublime.

It's a choice to sTay,
If it's all for the pay.
The life will experience an emotional array,
But life is too short to simply not treat it as a play.

"Never Really Behind"

It seems as if life has been given these numbers and at each one there are certain expectations.
Sometimes it be having traveled to a various amount of destinations,
Or creating special bonds and having other relations.

To this idea I have my oWn objection,
As I believe it leads to a life of personal negative reflection.
Some compare themselves to the others that live at another intersection,
Or the things they don't have wIthin their possession.
For the idea of want becomes an obsession.

See the life is not a rat chase,
Most certainly not a reckless drag race.
It's a complicated idea to fathom an infinite space.
So, one should feeL free to carry themselves at their own pace,
And not be ashamed of their own face.

The world can hold many scary things to find,
But one should never feel bad for trying to be kind.
Each individuaL should shine bright, as we are all never really behind.

"Perspective is the Objective"

Perspective is the objective,
And quite frankly it's suBjective,
As each mind is deceptive.
While all the people create what is known as the memory collective.

Test your might,
And bring life into sight,
For there's no need to fight.

It's what brings out emotion,
Then starts a commotion.
The population is much like a forever changing ocean.

To help see clear,
Look through the eyes of the one you hold dear,
And even the one you fear.
It will vastly change the dirEction you choose to steer.

It's a concept that drives the man mad,
Because his ideas aren't being had.

There can be peace in the world,
And the mind will be unfurled.

Only if one remembers that perspective,
Is everyone's objective.

"More Like Fiction Each Day"

"You've lost your miNd." Is what the people say,
As I express an idea that I whole heartedly portray.
This entire world is feeling morE like fiction each day,
It's becoming a life of infinite play.

I've taken the Grim thought of all actuality,
And brought it into the training realm of a forgotten practicality,
That's to reverse the idea of what's a dream and what's reaLity.

I believe you can be the grEatest perspective dream chaser,
As long as you maintain being a hopeful star gazer.
There wouldn't be a need to want to delete the past time with an imaginary eraser.

See now we'd have no need to reminisCe back to the days of our youth where our imaginaTion once flew,
And we were talking about the craziest of thIngs that we would do.
I've learNed to take the darkest of sky and turn it blue,
After takinG on this practice, all these outlandish ideas started to come true.
For I firmly believe, it can happen for you too.

"Snooze"

Snooze…
Hit it, if you so choose.

I must warn you, you chose your own fate,
And you're going to be laTe,
As you just entered a poor mental state.

Add to the fatigue,
But there's a wHole other league.

To play like the rest,
You must carry some zest.

Hop in your shoes,
If you so choose,
But it's your lifE to lose,
When you keep hitting snooze.

"Back Up to Five"

One can only look as far as The next bend,
For each new day the list seems to never Have an end,
As the new ideas continue to descend.

When one creates a list fOr the next rising sun,
Things must be completed for the next day of fUn.
Each one is checked off as it Gets done,
If not, forever live in a state of catching up to run.

Keep proceeding witH the list and the dreams will arrive,
No matter the different style of drive.
A set of words exist that let you know you're alive,
As the lisT of things to do will always go back up to five.

"Reflection on the Connection"

In order to make a reflection on the connection,
One must understand the idea of condemnation,
Is based sOlely on the situation.
As we live in this world of subjugation.

It seems that everyone has their own goal,
For there is always an idea that seems fitting in the heart of the soul.

It's like trying to deFine right or wrong,
Since there never is a correct variation of song.

To simply set the world free,
One must realize there is no difference between you and me.
All we want to do is make a world that we envision and see.

"Left Better on Paper"

Ever had a thought that would take a dusty thread from an unwoven tapestry and tried warp weaving it into a beautiful living life essence?
However, the ability of carrying out the action would have Meant complete control and being whole with nature's breathing presence.
The attempt contAined unharnessed power that sent the needle into a shifting arc that just didn't make sense,
For the weave is now a stitch with a permaNent unstable rift in the cosmic drIft that is ever so dense.
Now the actual result only supports the hold of what is now a mirrored reflection of a holograPhic iridescence.

The aftermath shows the repercussions of what wasn't ever sought,
And the land mUst get by with the very few strings it had horrendously caught.
For every plan that is mapped out to be perfect has no caLculations on the uncontrollable variable, and that would be the other beings natural reActing thought.

The passing of it all can transform what was a jusTifiable good willed intEntion just down to the grain of a taper.
As the experience from the many lessons learned will reaD,
"Sometimes things are just left better on paper."

"Tik Tok"

Tik Tok, Tik Tok,
Reality is built like a clock.
Tik Tok, Tik Tok,
The bones Will age to a rickety rock.
Tik TOk, Tik Tok,
Life is no diffeRent arounD the block.
Tik Tok, Tik Tok,
The ticking never stopS.

"City of Black and White"

What if I told you, I knew of a city that is black and white,
And it doesn't matter if it's day or night?

It is a place where the hearT is left on the floor,
Saying to yourself, "I don't want no more."

It's easy to say,
"Take it, just take it away!
I no longer want to live in this play,
Where all the walls are simply colored grey."

This city is populated by mOre than you think,
As we all have the same connecting data link.

To have lived in this city, I'll take just one token,
We all know what it's like to be heart broken.

"The Movement"

On a day to day life I disconnect,
And it's when I come inside to simply reflect,
That the stories and idEas can sometimes intersect.
Yet it turns me into a public test subject.

Put me on stage,
And I can calm your rage,
I'll show you how to flip your book of life to a new page.

I won't give you a hook and bass line,
Because we liVe in a world that is already lyrically defined,
I only want to take you on a trip inside your own mind.

This placE is a maze,
And it'll put you in a daze.
Take my hand and I'll show you the ways,
As we can change the woRld with onlY one phrase.

To create the universes greatest movement,
It all starts with internal self-improvement.

"Define a Black Hole"

To fully understand the definition of a black hole,
One must look inside the existing skull.

Its existence is only as strong as its slightest resistance,
And the idea of time is only relatiVe to the conception of distance.

The pupil is no different but the sAme,
As it absorbs all light into an infinite membRane.
We cannot define this since we call it the brain.

Be one with, or the mind will alwaYs dwell,
Creating the illusion of an intergalactic heaven or hell.
However, there will always exIst the flow of an even bigger swell.

So, open the soul to the inNer black door,
And only then will a being be able to soar.
Right into the inner core,
Where there is but nothinG more.

"To Diagnose a Personality"

To diagnose a personality,
Isn't it oh, the harshest of reality?
They've put descriptions on our life as if they can tell what's within our practicality.

Ever since the day of what was consiDered being a child,
There's some who say we're just a little too wild.
Now we have to conform to a world that seems too cautious and mild.

I'm here to say don't let diagnostic dEscriptive words define your life for we are all pioneers.
To the many that have not been claimed certain words, we will always be your bigGest fears.
Because we live a life of chasing those crowd winning cheers,
And envisioning that normal life just puts us in tears.

No matteR what they say,
We're going to chase a life of play.
All the way,
Until thE end of day.

So to the many that have been given those judgy trait names, we will all try,
Until we fly,
For our playground is the sky.
Human bEings we will always be, that is you and I.

"As They Please"

A simple fact will always remain True,
Every living tHing has something to do.
Whether it's flying solo, or in a crew,
That extravagant bEing is on a mission that it's going to pursue.

Everything is both weak yet stRong,
As sometimes the heartbeat is its only song.
So now its got lots of actions to perform to survive thE days of long.
Only then is it up to nature to decide if it was right or wrong.

This is just the way things Flow,
Much like the natural curves of a bow,
And to many, it's quite the idea to bestOw.

The universe of things cannot be changed with ease,
Such as a neveR ending wind some call the sea breeze.
Even we can't stop a squirrel that jumps to different trees,
Or the people that will always do as thEy please.

"Fiction is History"

Ever wonder why the people are so curious,
While the others are Taking their life way too serious?
Well it's because we are all delirious,
And don't know whether or not to travel inside a journey that is excitingly mysterious.

Now here's a secret to hold and conceal,
As this idea will be the biggest reveal…
That's to forget what's trutH and what's real.

The people will say this is the ultimate levEl of insanity,
However, the only rebuttal can be, it's a part of living inside our humanity.
For life is much prefeRably lived through the paperback face collecting dust on top of a vanity.

As to what's really happened in a life, it'll always be the greatest expressing inquiry.
That leaves us in a forevEr lost thinking state of an even bigger mystery,
And this is why it's claimed that all fiction is history.

"The Static"

The static,
Is something that is extremely problematic.

It has so many frequencies.
As it can change a person's consIstency,
And takes away from the feeling of really being free.

We still chose to connect to it,
Because it's an escape from this exact planet.

It will take you out of this realm,
But you're still the one at the helm.

To make a life that is leSs problematic,
One needs to disconnect from what we call the static.

"Judgement"

Some see it as the end of all things,
And that's exactly what the word brings,
As it takes away from the peace that the hummingbird sings.

Once oNe partakes in this action,
They've simply become a part of the condescending faction,
Thinking as if life has already determined a premeditated reaction.

It does not make the being any bolder,
In fact, it only turns the soul into a smolder.
As the world continues to get a little colder.

Choose to live in the moment,
And no longer be your only oppOnent,
Then eventually transcend into a positive exponent.

To live an everlasting life without repent,
Or bringing the body to a state of ferment,
One must live a life without the idea of judgement.

"7th Sense"

One always gets hilarity,
From another iNdividual's clarity.

It's not about who's above or below,
As when it comes to this it's everyone's show.

Take a deep breath and feel what's real,
For it's so inspiring, it sErves as its own meal.

If you just let it happEn,
Your wings will start flappin'.

It may seem like this worlD is so immense,
But it's easier to live in when you trust in the 7th sense.

"Are You Still in There?"

To coexist with change,
Is a feeling that is oh so strange,
It's that moment when the dial of life has been turned to the setting rearrange.

The journey is like searching over every single ridge,
Just to find the next crossing bridge.

The only thing found is the deepest Fear,
And that's for your physical being to not be here.
Now it's time to roam as a lonely musketeer,
Until we bOth become a part of the unknown clear.

I wouldn't have become who is the current standing me,
If we were never a buRning soulful we.
Now the wick of life has flickered down to a you and me.

Looking in the mirror while giving my curious eyes a very deep stare,
Wondering if there is but a single care.
I have to ask, "Are you still in there?"

"Slysdexic"

Tomesimes worbs get pedicted udside pown,
Where we 'tant cell what's ride sight up when we dook lown.

These lines create texravagAnt tilerature to peedly pexress one's
inner feelings of a life so greatly techic,
But writing it down makes the mind feel bervally ranoexic,
And tuilgy of pomclex thoughts because they deemed it slysdexic.

It makes life slightly mocplicated as certaiN things are wackbards,
While other metters lake fidderent worbs.

This grinbs up thoughts of needing nemtal poilet taper,
Or using it as a waY of freating the cinest of a written caper.

To get lost in the dwors is not a neakwess.
It's a great way of ckeching what the ceople pan miss,
As we need no tommunication when we toncain a deeper
unberstanbing of earths natural duiging pomcass.

"Cut the Line"

Here we go again; it's like we're living in this Place that we create,
All this animosity, discourage, and hate.

We string ouRselves up like we've been shackled and hooked,
It hits us so quick; we don't even have time to look.

We've tossed ourselves off the bOat,
It's this empty place where nothing can float.

This place you can drown,
Without being found.

Nobody will ever know,
Because you're living inside your own show.

You're looking around wondering,
Do I send myself Plundering?

For it all to be fine,
Do I even cut the line?

All it takes is one synapse,
To never again relapse.

It's your own crazy imagination of being scared.
You never even dared,
To sHow you cared,
So you kept to yourself, for fear of being compared.

It seems like if you speak the truth,
All of the suddEn you become bulletproof.

This is not true,
You beCome a slew.

So, all you have to do to be fine…
Is to simplY cut the line.

"Smirk Behind a Smile"

Let the warning be clear,
They aren't afraid of what's near.
As they've trained their mind to transcend fear,
And understand that their presence is simply being here.

While the others are seeing red,
Worried about what's being sAid,
The conscious aren't concerned about becoming the dead,
For they know their lineage has also once bled.

Learn to keep your composure,
And soon you'll be blind to the greatest of cynosure.
If one cannot, the life shall come to a very sad closure.

We are all living inside the human trial.
Be forewarned of the person who has no distance to their extra mile,
As these people are able to hide a Smirk behind a smile.

"To Weave the Sands of Time"

The easiest way to wipe the pain of it all,
Is to not forget to laugh as we all fall.
It eases to the thought of the speeds one can haul,
For the moment brings ticking time to a forever waiting stall.

Relativity of time is all based off the heart rate,
As well as the keen perspective of the carrier's weight.
The thought of that is on overdrive, so only the conscious can relate.

Learn to play with the floWing internal energy,
And grasp earths rotating movement as if it were a life auxiliary.
Then create what is to be the grandest of dual linking synergy.

There is an exponential trial before walking though the amber glowing gates,
Where the wildest of adventurer's destiny awaits.

Here one will receive a couple of knocks,
Decipher these to become the master of all mental locks,
And find a deEper understanding of a maniacal paradox.
This will shatter the mystical chains of pandora's box,
Which will allow the ability to stop all moving clocks.

To travel this journey is not a crime,
Nor would a person make a single dime.
It is merely harnessing the ability to weave the sands of time.

"Black or White"

In the evening when the sun creates a translucent burning sky,
There are some who release a grateful calming sigh,
While there are others who feel a need to let out a saddening cry.

Each person hAs a battle to choose to hide,
Or hop back up and decide to ride.
However, each individual's choice should be carried with pride.

To own these actions is neither wRong nor right,
As the passing day brings on a calm inspiring moonlight.
One looks up and dreams of flight,
While the other wondErs if things will ever be alright.
So remember to be kind, as we never know whose mind is dwelling in the black or white.

"The Application"

Here's the creation,
Of the application,
To give the peopLe the greatest unity sensation.
It would bring everyone humble satisfaction,
If we instilled hope to those who want to create positive tractiOn.

A couple of words on a paper don't even begin to describe what I've been through,
Or what I won't Stop at for what I'm willing to do.
So, let me flip your mind with a single thought or two.

Everyone that's conformed feels as if they know what it takes to ring the mIghtiest of bell,
Why not change the world by chasing the Nobel?

It would mean my ideas aren't putting people to work,
Just giving people perspective to be less of a jerk.

Instead of looking out simply look within,
Learn to be happy there to release that youthful cheesy grin.
If we all start with these we are Guaranteed to win,
As we bring on a shine for the world to want to continually spin.

"When it's Sunny and Snowing"

The universe is filled with magic moments that leave the mind in a blank state of unknowing,
As the lands enter a state that are seamlessly glOwing.
Then the phenomenon begins of when it's sunny and snowing.
It's quite impossible to fathom for there's never a single cloud even showing.

There will never be an explanation to the power that the land has broUght,
For everyone's soul became calm and carrying humble thought.
Now the search for unspeakable beauty was no longer a wish to be sought.
These are just some of the lessons that natuRe has taught,
As there is never nothing going on in any given spot.

"The Curtain Falls"

When the play is in the final chapter the greatest finale is the only thing left to contemplate,
So, if one can forget the deScription of a word it would mean the mightiest of swOrds no longer carries an edge or weight.
The holder of a pen wouldn't understand what's curved or what's straight,
And this idea would abolish the strongest of words suCh as love or hate.

Without any spoken voIce the ending would have nothing to say,
As the rest of the play,
Would be a physical display.
Many pEople would choose not to stay,
But the silent answer would hold the secret to what hides behind day.

Now as the silenT cheering of the audience calls,
Every living beings play is simplY waiting for when the curtain falls.

www.ingramcontent.com/pod-product-compliance
Lightning Source LLC
Chambersburg PA
CBHW060045230426
43661CB00004B/662